ART UP THIS JOURNAL

An artistic way to have fun with journaling in your everyday life

This book was made because some days are just no
Fun and we need a way to relax and enjoy it.
Journaling can help get your feelings out but now
With art it can be even more enjoyable.☺

Tamara L Adams

Please leave a review ☺
Indie Writers Depend on Reviews!

Contact T L. Adams

Tammy@tamaraladamsauthor.com
tamaraadamsauthor@gmail.com
www.tamaraladamsauthor.com
https://twitter.com/@TamaraLAdams
https://www.facebook.com/TamaraLAdamsAuthor/
http://www.amazon.com/T.L.-Adams/e/B00YSROGC4
https://www.pinterest.com/Tjandlexismom/tamara-l-adams-author/

Copyright © 2016 Tamara L Adams
All rights reserved. No part of this publication may be reproduced,
distributed, or transmitted in any form
or by any means, including photocopying, recording,
or other electronic or mechanical methods,
without the prior written permission of the publisher, except in the
case of brief quotations embodied in reviews and certain other
non-commercial uses permitted by copyright law.

Table of Contents: Page# and prompt

Find a prompt that pertains to your mood
Go to that prompt within the book.
Have fun and make art according to that prompt.

1. Draw something positive .....
2. Cover the page with random objects..
3. Draw something for a stranger...
4. Create a mantra...
5. Make a picture starting with this half circle....
6. Draw a happy scene...
7. Staple money to this page...
8. Draw the best sunset....
9. Make your own Mandala....
10. Draw your best personality trait...
11. Make a paper airplane...
12. Draw your favorite book...
13. Trace your hand then decorate it...
14. Create a picture from this triangle....
15. Draw your favorite holiday...
16. Connect the dots on this page...
17. Draw your mood right now.....
18. Make a football ...
19. Draw random lines...
20. Freeze this page...
21. Draw a stick person scene...
22. Make art out of the half heart..
23. Glue newspaper clippings here......
24. Draw a nature scene...

25. Draw a maze...
26. Make art with only circles...
27. Create your own map...
28. Draw smiles all over...
29. Make a collage...
30. Finish the half circle...
31. Draw flowers all over...
32. Draw an ice cream or candy world...
33. Draw your favorite outfit...
34. Make a hidden objects picture...
35. Draw a beach scene...
36. Design a crest for your family...
37. Make art out of the shape...
38. Draw the perfect flower...
39. Design your dream home ...
40. Make a word search...
41. Draw a picture without lifting your pen ...
42. Melt crayons onto the page...
43. Draw furniture layouts for a room in your house...
44. Design a tattoo...
45. Draw your favorite pet or animal...
46. Make art out of the object (stop sign)...
47. Design jewelry ...
48. Make your own dot-to-dot...
49. Draw with your eyes closed...
50. Design your own fortune teller...

Have fun! ☺

Prompt 1:

DRAW SOMETHING POSITIVE ON THIS PAGE

THEN HANG IT ON YOUR WALL.

Prompt 2:

COVER THIS PAGE WITH RANDOM OBJECTS USING ONLY YOUR FAVORITE COLOR

Prompt 3:

DRAW SOMETHING NICE AND GIVE IT TO A STRANGER

Prompt 4:

Create a mantra (statement or slogan), add art to it

Prompt 5:

Make a picture starting with this half-circle

Prompt 6:

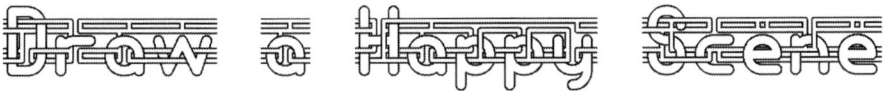

Prompt 7:

STAPLE MONEY
ONTO THIS PAGE
AND LEAVE IT IN A
PUBLIC PLACE
TO MAKE SOMEONE'S DAY

Prompt 8:

Prompt 9:

MAKE YOUR OWN MANDALA

Prompt 10:

Draw your best personality trait

Prompt 11:

Make a Paper airplane

Prompt 12:

Draw your favorite Book

Prompt 13:

Trace your hand

And
Decorate
it

Prompt 14:

Finish the drawing

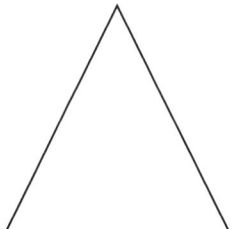

Prompt 15:

Draw your favorite holiday

Prompt 16:

Connect the dots on this page however you want

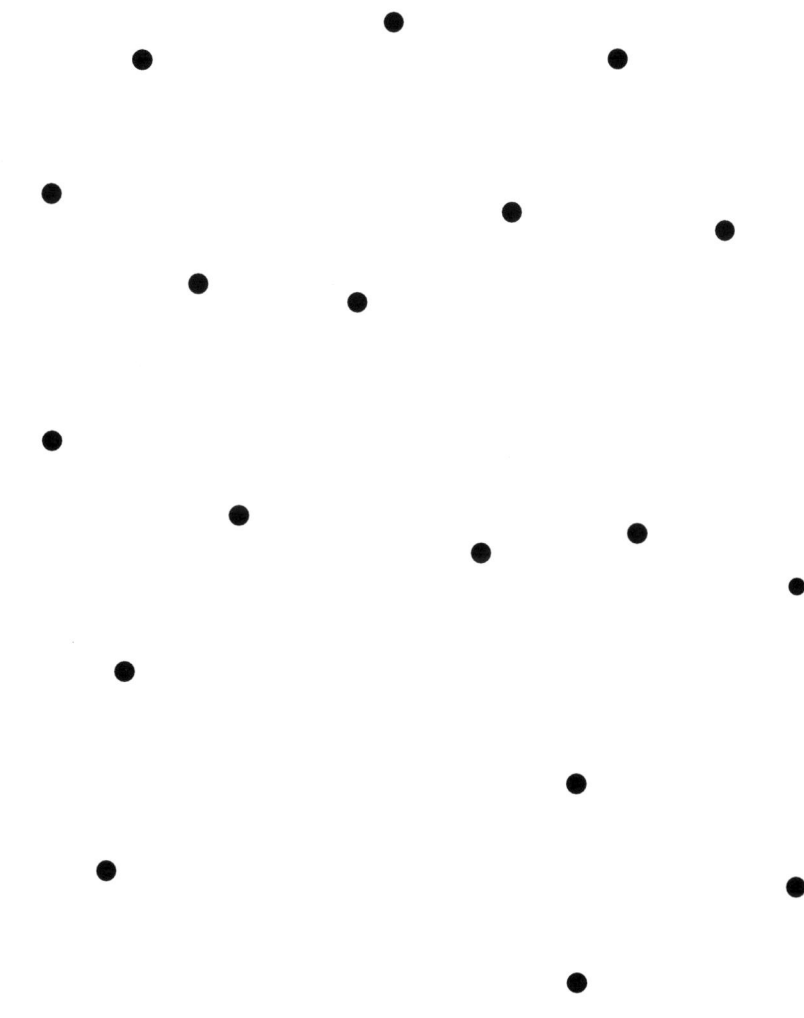

Prompt 17:

DRAW YOUR MOOD RIGHT NOW

Prompt 18:

Make a football out of this page and play a game

DRAW RANDOM LINES ALL OVER THIS PAPER

Prompt 19:

Prompt 20:

FIND A WAY TO FREEZE THIS PAGE

Prompt 21:

DRAW A STICK PERSON SCENE

Prompt 22:
Finish the drawing

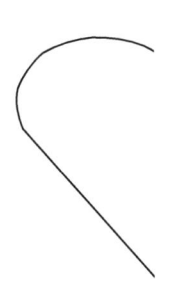

Prompt 23:

Glue newspaper clippings all over this page

Prompt 24:

DRAW A NATURE SCENE

Prompt 25:

TRY TO DRAW A MAZE

Prompt 26: Draw a picture using only circles

Prompt 27: Create your own map

Prompt 28:

Draw several different smiles *all over the page*

Prompt 29:

Make a collage on this page

Prompt 30:

Finish the drawing

Prompt 31:

```
        F
        L
        O
   D    W         O    T    P
   R    E    A    V    H    A
   A    R    L    E    I    G
   W    S    L    R    S    E
```

Prompt 32:

Draw an Ice cream or candy world

Prompt 33:

draw your favorite outfit

Prompt 34: Make a Hidden Objects Theme

Prompt 35:

DRAW A BEACH SCENE

Prompt 36: Design a crest for your family name

Prompt 37:

Finish the drawing

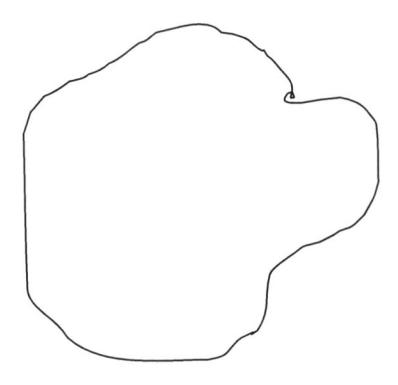

Prompt 38:

Draw the perfect flower

Prompt 39:

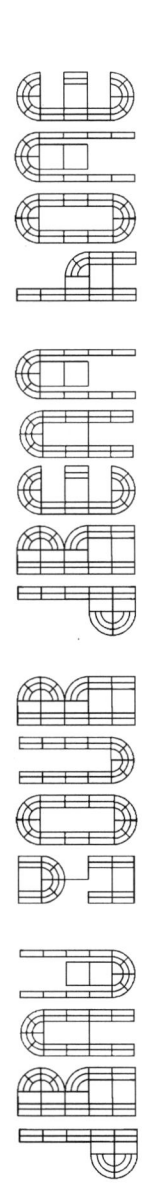

Prompt 40:

Make your own word search

Prompt 41:

DRAW A PICTURE WITHOUT TAKING YOUR PEN/PENCIL OFF THE PAPER

Prompt 42:

MELT CRAYONS WITH A CANDLE AND DRIP ONTO THIS PAGE

Prompt 43:

DRAW A ROOM IN OUR HOUSE WITH DIFFERENT FURNITURE LAYOUT OPTIONS

Prompt 44:

Design a tattoo you could get

Prompt 45:

Draw your favorite pet that you have or want

Prompt 46:
$\mathcal{F}$inish the drawing

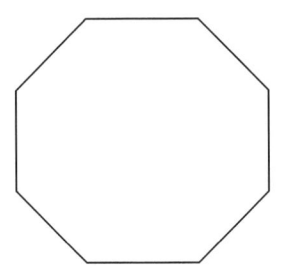

Prompt 47:

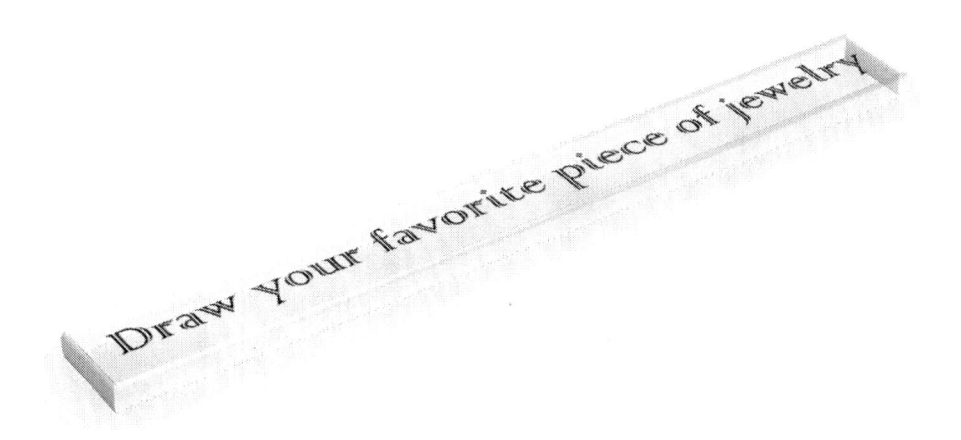

Draw your favorite piece of jewelry

Prompt 48:

Make
Your
Own dot-to-dot

Prompt 49:

Draw with your Eyes closed

Prompt 50:

Design your own fortune teller

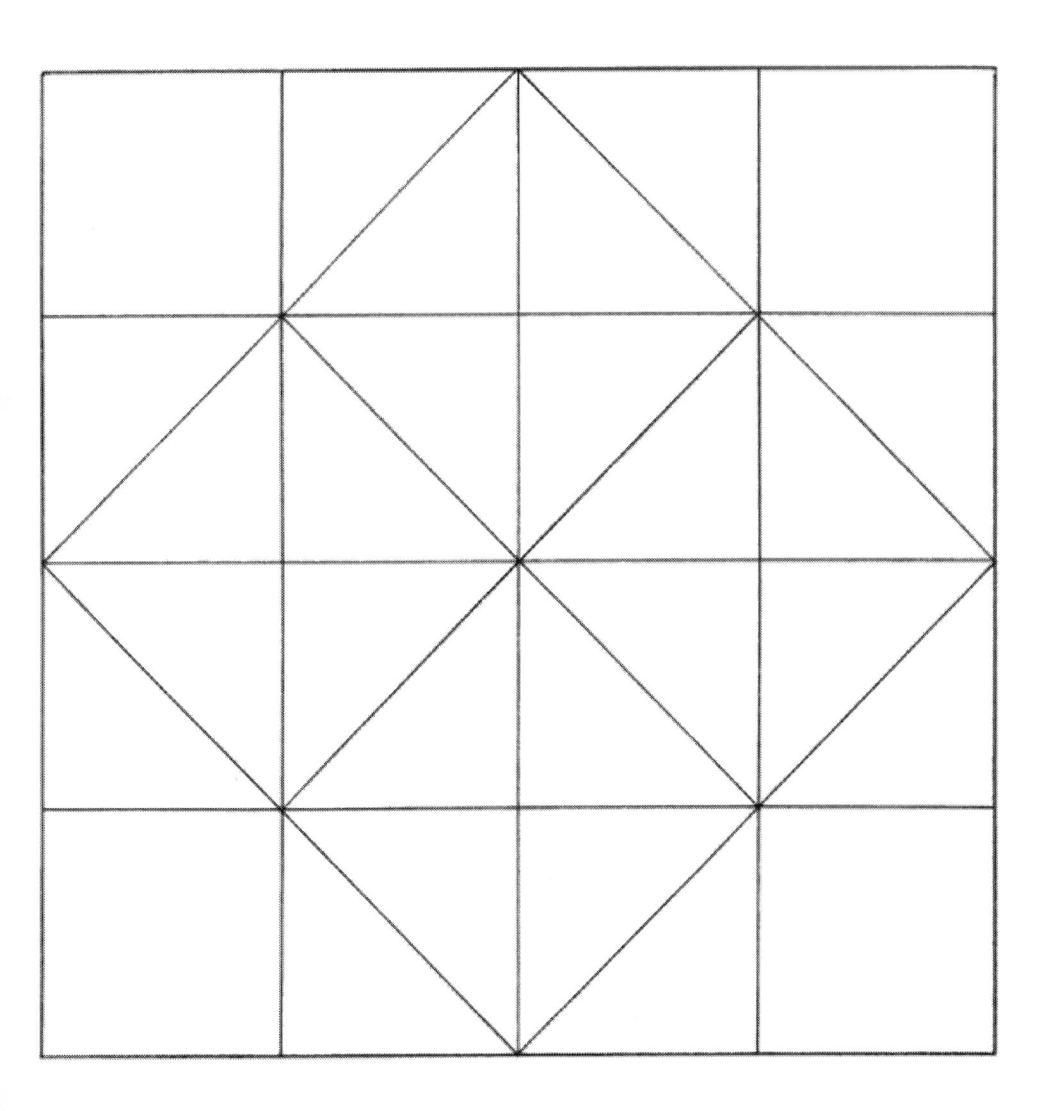

Please leave a review ☺
Indie Writers Depend on Reviews!

Contact Tamara L. Adams:

Tammy@tamaraladamsauthor.com

tamaraadamsauthor@gmail.com

www.tamaraladamsauthor.com

https://twitter.com/@TamaraLAdams

https://www.facebook.com/TamaraLAdamsAuthor/

http://www.amazon.com/T.L.-Adams/e/B00YSROGC4

https://www.pinterest.com/Tjandlexismom/tamara-l-adams-author/

Here are some of my other Journals!

Made in the USA
Monee, IL
27 November 2019